CHRISTMAS

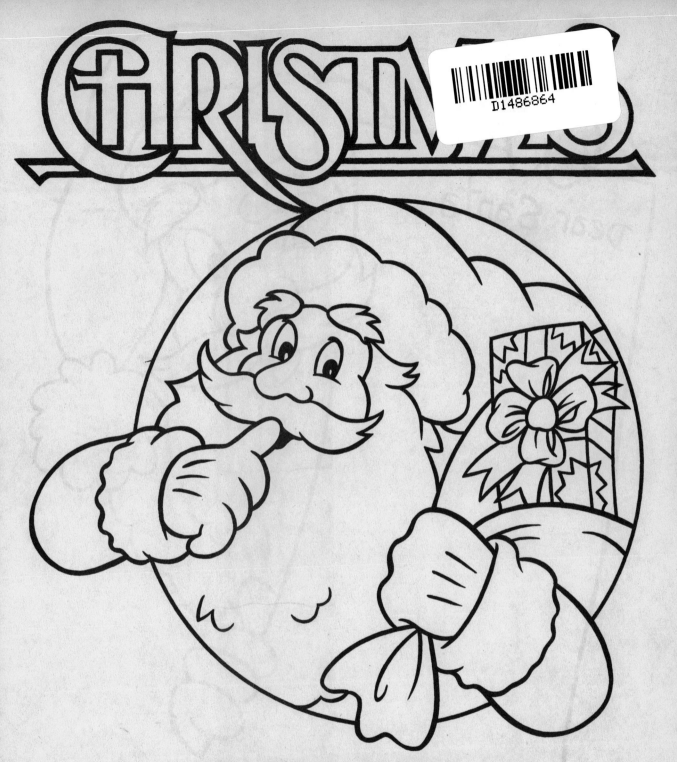

Illustrated by Lance Raichert

Published by

Pyramid Publishing

P.O. Box 129

Zenda, Wisconsin 53195

Dear Santa...

Finish the letter to Santa.

Color the picture.

Draw a face on Santa.

**Color the shapes with a dot in it to see
what Santa is saying.**

How many Santa hats can you count ?

Find the 5 things that are different between the two drawings.

Finish the drawing.

Finish the drawing.

START

NORTH POLE

FINISH

Help the elf get to the North Pole.

Find the 5 things that are different between
the two drawings.

Color the picture.

Connect the dots.

Follow the lines to the correct match.

Draw the **Wreath** Using the grid.

**Find 5 things that are different between
the two drawings.**

How many snowflakes are there ?

Color the drawing.

Draw a line to the right shadow.

Draw the **Christmas Star** Using the grid.

Follow the lines to the correct match.

Draw a face on the elf.

Circle the one that doesn't belong.

How many flowers are there?

Draw the **Christmas Flower** Using the grid.

Finish the snow flake.

Color the picture.

Find the 5 things that are different between the two drawings.

Color the shapes with a dot in it to see
what the Snowman wants.

Draw the **Candle** Using the grid.

Follow the lines to the correct match.

Color the picture.

Draw a line to the right shadow.

Finish the drawing.

How many bows are there ?

Find the 5 things that are different between the two drawings.

Draw the bird of peace.

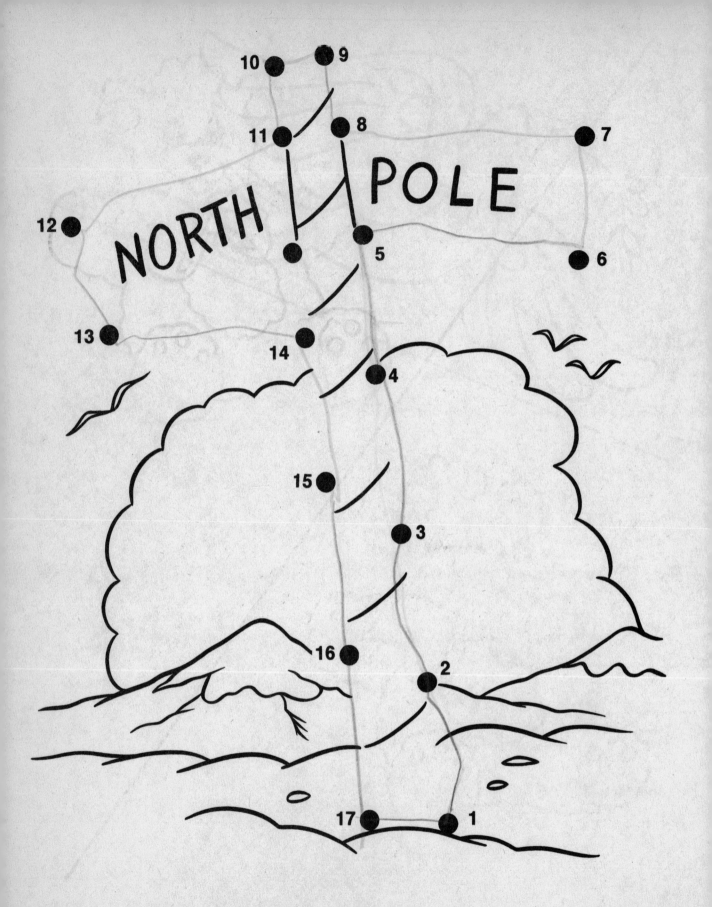

NORTH POLE

Connect the dots.

**Find the 5 things that are different between
the two drawings.**

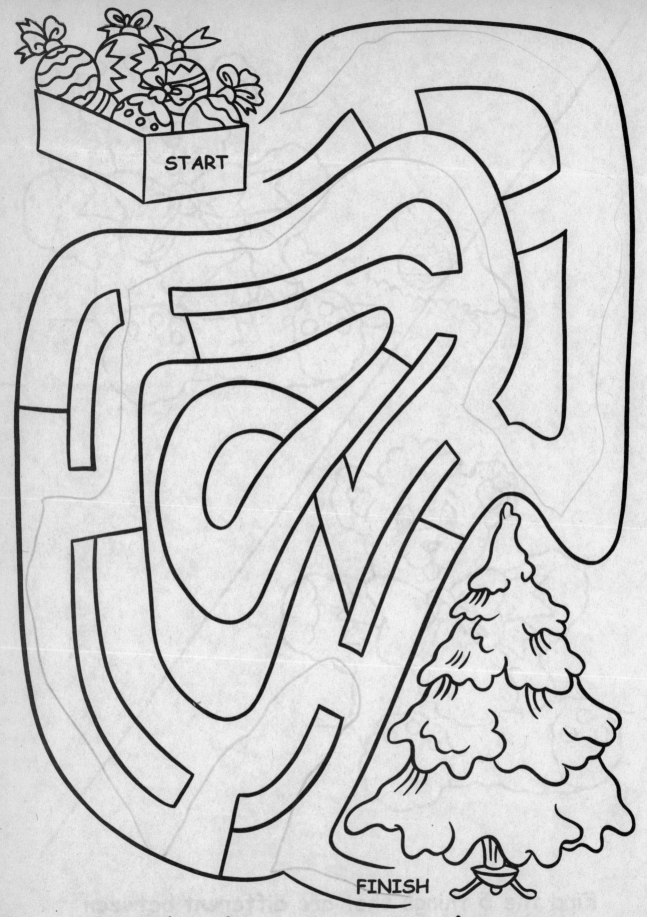

START

FINISH

Get the decorations to the tree.

Finish the drawing.

Decorate the tree.

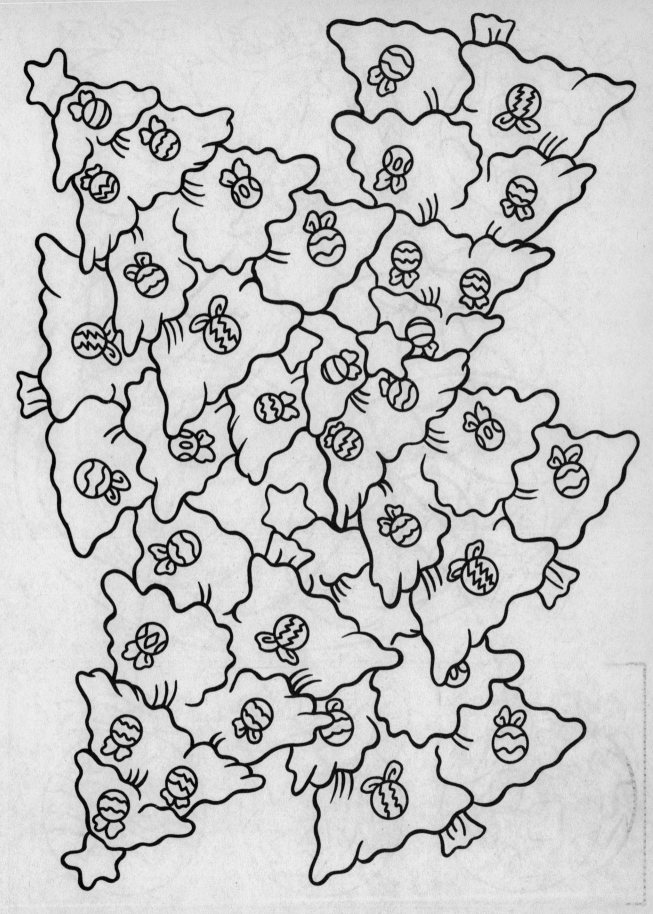

How many Christmas trees are there ?

Follow the lines to the correct match.

START

FINISH

Help the reindeer get to the sleigh.

Finish the drawing.

Draw **Horn** Using the grid.

How many snow men are there ?

Circle the one that doesn't belong.

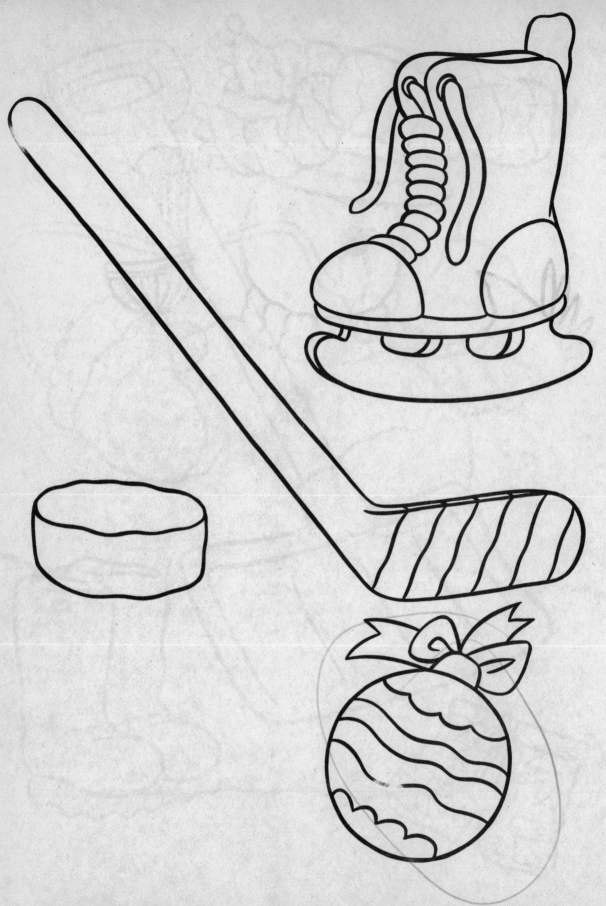

Circle the one that doesn't belong.

Finish the drawing.

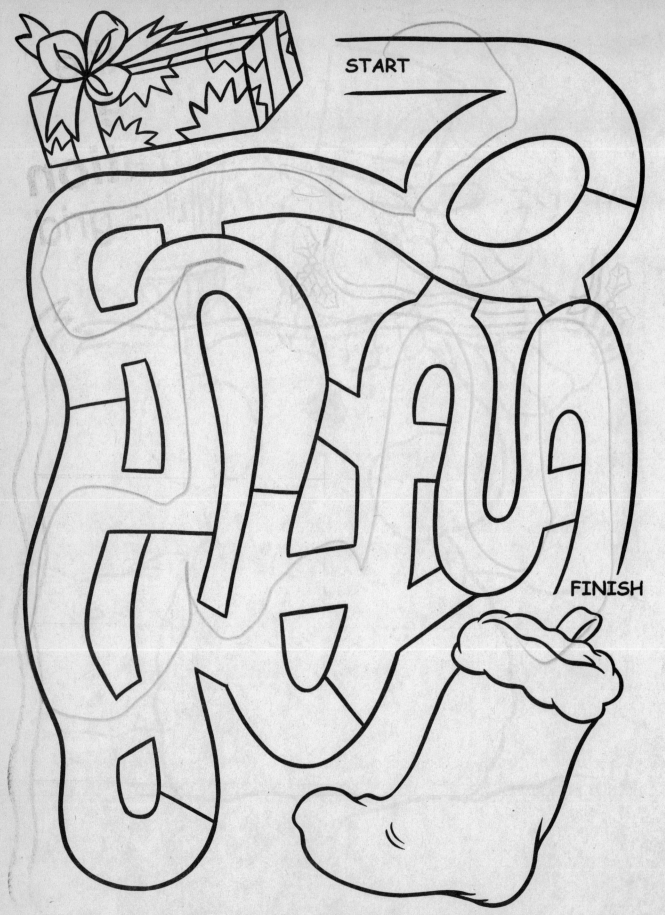

START

FINISH

Put the gift in the stocking.

Draw the **Tree Decoration** Using the grid.

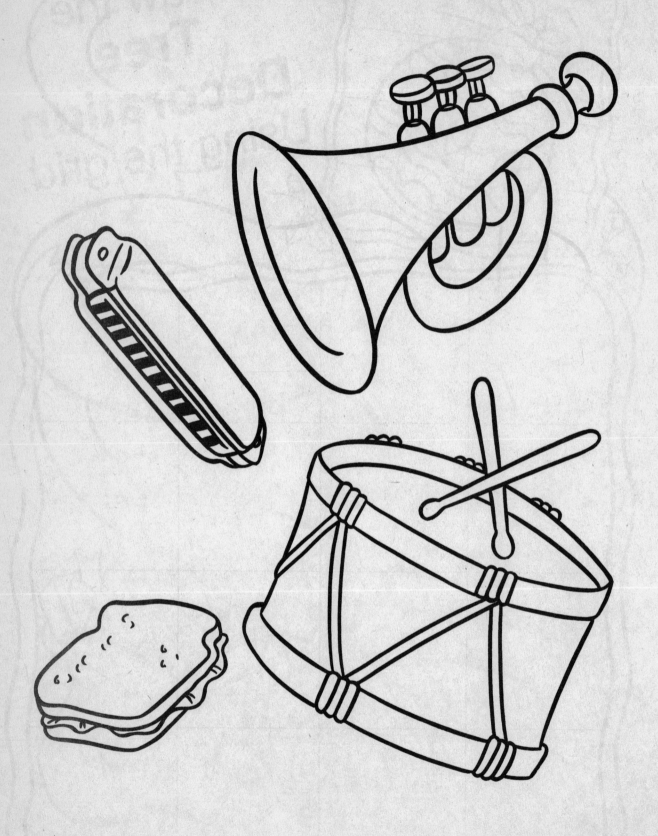

Circle the one that doesn't belong.

START

FINISH

Help Santa get to his toys.

Find the 5 things that are different between the two drawings.

Finish the drawing.

Draw the **Doll** Using the grid.

Draw **Bell** Using the grid.

Finish the drawing.

Color the picture.

Color the picture.

THANK YOU

Santa

Color the picture.